Spotlight on

The English Revolution

Julia Newhouse and
Jan King

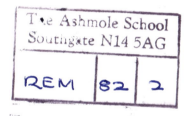
Cassell Graded Readers Level 6

General Editor: Michael Carrier

Cassell

Lond

CASSELL LTD
35 Red Lion Square, London WC1R 4SG
an affiliate of
Macmillan Publishing Co Inc
New York

First published 1982

British Library Cataloguing in Publication Data

Newhouse, Julia
    Spotlight on the English Revolution. − (Spotlight
    readers)
    1. English language − Text-books for foreigners
    2. Readers − Great Britain − History − Puritan
    Revolution
    I. Title   II. King, Jan
    428.6′4   PE1127.H/

ISBN 0 304 30571 5

Printed in Hong Kong by Wing King Tong Printing Co. Ltd.

Illustrations by Paul Blount (9, 13, 21, 47, 51, 58, 62)
and Anna Read (63)

Our thanks are due to the following for permission to
reproduce photographs:
National Portrait Gallery (2, 28, 33, 60)
Fotomas Index (17, 46, 70)
British Tourist Authority (35, 37, 41, 66)

942. 06

Contents

CASSELL GRADED READERS

ELEMENTARY

Spotlight on

Level 1
(350 headwords)
- A Doctor's Day
- Illusions
- Muhammad Ali
- A Radio Station

Level 2
(700 headwords)
- The Beginning of Radio
- Inventions
- British Food
- Tennis

INTERMEDIATE

Spotlight on

Level 3
(1050 headwords)
- Motor Racing
- Football
- The Kennedys
- The Common Market

Level 4
(1400 headwords)
- Surprises of Nature
- Fleet Street
- William Shakespeare
- Strange Stories

ADVANCED

Spotlight on

Level 5
(1750 headwords)
- British Theatre
- The Pop Industry

Level 6
(2100 headwords)
- The English Revolution
- Winston Churchill

Preface

This is a new series of readers for foreign students of English. It is new in several ways. Firstly, it has been designed as a series rather than an arbitrary group of titles. Secondly, the series provides reading material that is representative of the students' interests and corresponds as far as possible to the books that students would read in their own language. Thus it consists only of informative, entertaining, non-fiction topics. Thirdly, the language used in the readers has been carefully chosen and controlled so as to be easily understandable for students without being childish or patronising in its tone. At the same time each reader introduces a sizeable amount of subject-specific vocabulary which would not normally be included in a simple grading system. This subject-specific vocabulary is carefully explained through text, illustration or glossary so that the student can deal with topics in a more serious and informative way.

There are six levels, Level 1 being the simplest and Level 6 the most difficult. Each level introduces *circa* 350 new headwords and the length of each reader depends on its level (cf. list of titles at the beginning of this book).

The language is controlled lexically according to a grading system, and subject-specific vocabulary is added where appropriate. There is also a structural grading which keeps syntactic complexity to a level that is comprehensible to the student. This operates mainly in Levels 1–4.

As one of the main aims of Cassell's Graded Readers is to stimulate the students' interest and motivation to read, the books are presented in a lively and interesting format and are well illustrated throughout. Each book also contains follow-up exercises and activities to give students the opportunity to take their interest in the topic, as well as in the language, further than a merely passive reading of the text.

Further details of the linguistic grading can be found in the Teachers' Guide to the series, obtainable from the publishers.

Colchester, 1982

Michael Carrier
General Editor

1
The beginnings of the problem

One bitterly cold morning in London in January 1649, a man was brought out of his prison. The time had come for him to die. The man was wearing two shirts so that he did not shiver* from the cold. If the people that came to see him die saw him shivering, he thought, they might think he was afraid; and he intended to die bravely. He fell on his knees in front of the block*, said his prayers and prepared to die. A great crowd stood watching as the axe* descended* and cut off his head — the head of King Charles I of England.

Charles I became King in the year 1625 but to understand the problems and arguments that led to his death we must go back a further hundred years to the time of King Henry VIII.

When Henry became King in 1509, England was a Roman Catholic* country, with the Pope* in Rome as the head of the Church. The Roman Catholic Church does not allow divorce. Henry's problems began when he decided he wanted to divorce his wife, Catherine of Aragon. Catherine had not given Henry a son to become King in his place and by this time she was 42 years old. So he wished to divorce her and make Anne Boleyn

* See Glossary
    New words are asterisked (*) the first time they occur only.

Henry VIII

his new queen. He asked the Pope's permission to do this but when the Pope refused to give him permission, Henry decided to disobey him and declared that the Church in England would no longer recognise the Pope as its leader. He then set himself up as the head of the Church of England.

It was an unhappy time for those people in England who wanted to remain in the Roman Catholic Church. Henry demanded that everyone obey him and accept him as the head of the Church of England on pain of death. He believed in the Divine* Right of Kings. According to this law, anyone who criticised the Church was also criticising the King, and anyone who spoke against the King was also speaking against God.

During this period, Henry VIII was not the only person who felt angry with the Roman Catholic Church. New ideas were spreading across Europe where people were also questioning the power of the Pope and these ideas led to the birth of Protestantism*, so called because its followers protested against the authority* of the Pope. Many poor people in England turned against the Roman Catholic Church because of its great wealth which did not seem fair to them. A lot of other people, however, did not want to change their form of religion. They believed in the Pope as the head of the Church and could not accept Henry as their religious leader.

However, things did not stay like this for long. From then on each new king or queen of England decided which form of religion the country would follow. When the Roman Catholic queen Mary Tudor, came to the throne* in 1553 the Protestants suffered persecution* under her. Many were thrown into prison and tortured* and some were even burnt to death.

Queen Elizabeth I, who came to the throne in 1558, was a Protestant. During her reign*, the Roman Catholics were persecuted. There was no religious freedom in England and the Catholics and Protestants hated each other more and more.

Protestants and Puritans

In about 1600 a new kind of Protestantism, called Puritanism, was growing in England. The Puritans were very 'pure', serious people who believed it was wrong to dance, sing, play music or take part in sports on Sunday. They thought people should go to church, read their Bibles* and sit quietly at home and that it was wrong to laugh or to wear brightly coloured clothes. The Puritans wanted to organise their own church with their own leaders but Queen Elizabeth would not allow this. Nor was Parliament happy about its own position in relation to the Queen. Members of Parliament* felt that Elizabeth had too much power and they wanted more for themselves.

The problem was now growing more complicated. A hundred years before there had been one religion and a King who everyone obeyed without question. Now there were three different kinds of Christian* in England: the Roman Catholics, the Protestants and the Puritans. There was also the problem of Parliament growing tired of the unlimited powers of the monarch*.

After Elizabeth I died in 1603, the Protestant King James I, who was already King of Scotland, came to the English throne. He did nothing to improve the situation for Roman Catholics and a group of them planned to murder him and most of his Members of Parliament by blowing up the Houses of Parliament while he was there. But the plan was discovered and one of the Catholics, a man called Guy Fawkes, was found in the cellars* and was arrested and tortured. In those days the English tortured people who were suspected of doing wrong and poor Guy Fawkes had his thumbs slowly pulled apart by a terrible instrument of torture. He then had his head cut off by the executioner's* axe. Although this was the plan of only a few men, it made the Protestants hate the Roman Catholics even more.

King James was a clever but very proud man who did not get on well with people. No-one could talk about or discuss things with him. Also he gave positions of power to his favourites, many of whom came from Scotland. This did not please Parliament. One day he told Parliament that, as England was short of money, his son, Prince Charles, should marry a rich, Spanish princess. Parliament, however, did not agree with the King because Spain was a Roman Catholic country. James was furious* with this reply and many Members of Parliament were thrown into prison. Those who remained began to hate James.

The political situation was bad and the religious difficulties grew. The Puritans were suffering, many going to prison and even dying for their beliefs. Some Puritan families escaped by sailing away to America where they were able to start a new life. A group of 100 Puritans, known as the Pilgrim Fathers*, sailed to America in 1620 in order to break away completely from the Church of England.

When James died in 1625 and his son, Charles, became King, England was neither a peaceful nor a happy country. The sky was growing dark and the power struggle between the different religious and political groups would soon lead to civil* war; the storm was about to break over England.

2
Parliament is dismissed*

Under King Charles I the situation grew worse. When Charles came to the throne England was at war at sea with Spain and Parliament felt the war was being badly run. Their complaints were aimed at the Duke of Buckingham who was in charge of the Navy (the army of the sea). As Buckingham was Charles' best friend and adviser, they were therefore also criticising the King. Buckingham started several wars which failed, so wasting a lot of money. He had also arranged Charles' marriage to the Roman Catholic French princess* Henrietta Maria who was to cause England many problems.

Eventually Buckingham was murdered by a Puritan extremist* to the great joy of the people. Charles, because of lack of money, stopped organising wars but he still wanted to govern without Parliament. Finally the Members of Parliament wrote a long list of all the things they disliked about what Charles was doing, called the 'Petition* of Rights'. This gave Charles the excuse he wanted to dismiss Parliament and try governing the country alone.

The leader of Parliament was a man called John Eliot who had hated the Duke of Buckingham and had often spoken out against him. When Parliament was dismissed he was put in prison in the Tower because he supported the Petition of Rights but Charles was especially hard on him because of the death of Buckingham.

For three years Eliot lived in a little, dark room before he eventually died. The English people were very angry at his death for Eliot had been popular. He was one of the few people who had been brave enough to speak out against the King.

Charles now needed a lot more public money and he decided to make people pay more taxes. The most famous of these taxes was Ship Money. Until this time, only people who lived in ports had had to pay it so that their ships would be looked after. It was a tax for the protection of their ships. Now Charles decided that everyone should have to pay Ship Money.

But John Hampden, who had been John Eliot's best friend, said that such a tax would be against the law and many people refused to pay it. Some were thrown into prison for refusing to pay and some were tortured with cruel and painful instruments. Others decided it was easier to pay than to protest.

By now Charles was angry and rather frightened. So many people were against him that he felt he had to show his power and authority by keeping the people down and showing them that he was King.

In 1637 Charles felt that the Puritans were beginning to do what they wanted in religious matters. He decided that this had to stop. They must be made to obey the Church of England, the King's Church. He ordered them to sing and dance on Sundays and to stop trying to prevent other people from enjoying themselves. They were to follow the religion of the Church of England and not interfere with what other people did.

However, many Puritans continued to practise their own kind of religion and continued to criticise people who enjoyed themselves on Sundays. They held public meetings. Charles was angry to find that they were not obeying him and several Puritans had their ears cut off because they did not give up their faith.

A lot of Puritans left England and travelled abroad to live. Many of them went to avoid persecution although

A Puritan couple

several left in order to have more land for their large families. Some went for the adventure and perhaps hoping to find gold and silver mines as the Spanish had found in Mexico and Peru. Others wanted to trade and become rich through business.

In Scotland the Puritans were even more angry with the King. Charles wanted them to accept a new prayer-book written by Archbishop* Laud who was the most important religious leader under Charles I.

One Sunday in Scotland, a church leader was reading from the new prayer-book, which everybody hated, when an angry young woman picked up a chair and threw it at the man. He was very frightened and ran from the church with a crowd of angry people shouting after him.

Many rich Scots also hated Charles because he forced them to pay a lot of money in taxes. They wanted their own Scottish Parliament and were tired of the English Church and its King. Thousands of Scots, rich and poor, Puritan and non-Puritan, came together and formed an army to fight against the King.

3
Charles and the Earl* of Stafford

Charles now realised he had to get an army together to fight the Scots but armies cost money and Charles had no money. So in 1640 he called Parliament together to ask for some money. This Parliament had a very short life, however, as it insisted that it had a duty to govern the country and Charles would not agree to this.

Charles succeeded in getting together a small army which marched to Scotland although none of the soldiers really wanted to fight. The officers complained that the Scots had a stronger army and the English had no money. They did not want to fight the Scots and so there was no battle. Charles was angry with the Scots but even more angry with his own army. Nobody was obeying him any longer; he seemed to be losing his power.

Finally Charles called his adviser, Thomas Wentworth, to ask what he should do and Wentworth advised him to call a new Parliament. He told the King to demand money from the new Parliament and bring an army from Ireland to fight the Scots. Wentworth, who was governing Ireland for Charles, was eventually made Earl of Stafford. Ship taxes were increased to get more money and armies from Italy and France were asked to help fight the Scots.

When Charles' plans were known, the people of England and Scotland were extremely angry. The King was using their money to bring in foreign armies that he wanted to use against some of his own people. By this time almost everybody was against Charles and also against Archbishop Laud and the Earl of Stafford, who was leader of the King's army.

People grew more and more discontented and there was fighting in the streets of London. The City Aldermen*, the men who looked after the public money, refused to give Charles any more money for the war against Scotland.

Stafford advised Charles to hang some of those who had been fighting, as an example, so that the people would see what would happen if they did not obey the King. Then a group of Londoners attacked Laud's home and he had to run away and hide. Many of those who had been in the fighting were tortured on the rack* by being stretched until their bones broke and then they were hanged. (It is thought that this was the last time the rack was used as an instrument of torture but it can still be seen today at Madame Tussaud's in London.)

In 1640 Charles moved his army to the north of England. He was very short of both money and men. The Scottish army crossed into England where the two armies met — but Charles' army did not want to fight yet again. So, of course, the Scots won the battle and now controlled part of the north of England. They made

The rack

Charles give them £850 a day, which was a lot of money in those days, to pay for the Scottish army.

The King called together a Parliament in November 1640. John Pym, a very popular leader, spoke with great courage against the Earl of Stafford. He said Stafford had betrayed* the people of England and acted against their interests. Many Englishmen had died because of him and Pym said he should be brought to trial in a court of law.

Stafford was found guilty and put in prison in the Tower of London. Charles was very upset. Parliament wanted Stafford's death and Charles had to sign the death warrant* giving official permission. A few weeks

later Stafford was beheaded* and Laud was put to death
not long afterwards. The two biggest enemies of England were now dead. Parliament had shown its strength
and authority at last.

Many social improvements followed these events and
the rules for governing the country were completely
changed. Some people thought these changes were too
extreme but felt anything was better than the way the
country had been governed before. There were, however, violent Roman Catholic protests in Ireland where
the Church said that Parliament was acting against the
law and against the wishes of God.

Charles was not sure what to do next. He invited Pym
to become a member of the King's personal government
at the Treasury* — the part of the government that
decides how the Government's money is to be collected,
and spent — in order to keep an eye on him, but Pym
refused. Charles then decided it was time he showed
Parliament that the power was still in his hands. He
planned to arrest John Pym, John Hampden and three
other men who were causing all his difficulties and he
decided to arrest these five men himself.

He was rather nervous of walking into Parliament
alone, for he knew everyone there hated him, so he took
500 soldiers with him. But the five Members he had
come to arrest were no longer in the House as someone
had warned them of their danger. The five had escaped
by boat along the River Thames and had hidden with
friends in the City of London where they felt safe from
the King.

It was clear by now that only war would decide who should govern. The whole country was divided: there were those who were on the King's side and felt that Charles, as King, ought to govern and that everyone should obey him; and there were those who were on the side of Parliament who felt that the country should be governed by representatives of the people to protect the people.

The first big political revolution of modern times was beginning. It was going to become a bitter civil war.

4
The Battle of Edgehill

In January 1642, after King Charles had tried to arrest them, the people of London hid Pym, Hampden and their friends and looked after them. These people were frightened that King Charles would send an army to fight them because they were sheltering the King's enemies but Charles himself was also frightened. So many of his people now stood against him that, instead of fighting, he decided to run away and abandon* the throne, at least temporarily*.

His wife, Queen Henrietta Maria, escaped to Holland taking one of their children with her. The Queen was a strong, determined woman who had often told Charles what to do. Indeed it was she who had told Charles to arrest Pym and the other four men.

King Charles and his eldest son, the young Prince* Charles, went north into Yorkshire where they hoped the people would be on their side. The Scottish army had now returned to Scotland and Charles hoped to find things peaceful. He was mistaken, though, for when he arrived at the north east coastal town of Hull, the Governor of the town came out and shouted from the city walls for the King to go away. Charles, seeing he was not welcome, decided to take his 1,000 men away and they left for Nottingham, a town in central England. He and his relatively* small army camped there and Charles set up his court.

At this time Parliament made the mistake of declaring that anyone who supported the King would have their property and possessions taken away. Naturally this made many people, especially the rich, afraid of the Parliamentarians. They now felt that the only way to protect their interests was to join forces and fight with the King. So people who had not yet made up their minds, mostly those who had property to lose, now decided to fight for the King.

When the first big battle of the English Civil War was fought at Edgehill near Oxford, the King had quite a large army because people were becoming unhappy with Parliament. At this time there were many small battles being fought all over England but they did not

last long because both sides soon tired of fighting. The farmers wanted to return to their farms, for there was a lot of work to be done, and the Londoners wanted to return to the town, away from the difficult conditions of army camps in the country.

One of the main fighters on the King's side was his nephew, Prince Rupert, who wore bright red clothes and for some strange reason always took his little white dog with him into battle. One of the most important fighters on the side of Parliament was Captain Oliver Cromwell, a brave soldier and a cousin of John Hampden — one of Pym's friends who had escaped by boat from the King.

The King and his son stood and watched the fighting at Edgehill but did not take part. One of Charles' faithful followers, Sir Edmund Verney, was killed during the battle, which made the King very sad. Every night both sides stopped fighting and tried to sleep but the wounded were screaming with pain, there was blood everywhere and on some nights it was bitterly cold. The skill of the army doctors in looking after wounded men was very limited and often men's arms or legs would be cut off without any anaesthetic*. In many cases, the doctors could do nothing and so the men died very slowly and in great pain as no painkilling drugs were known in the 17th century.

Finally both sides grew tired of fighting. They were tired of seeing all the blood and of hearing all the screams of dying men. The Parliamentarian army stopped fighting first but both sides claimed they had won the battle and so no decision was agreed on.

5
Oliver Cromwell

Oliver Cromwell was born in Huntingdon in 1599 and grew up on a large farm. His uncle, Sir Oliver Cromwell, was an important and rich man whom King James I sometimes visited. On one visit he brought his son, Prince Charles, with him and Charles and Oliver were sent into the garden to play. They fought with each other, as boys often do, and Oliver won. Neither then knew that they would be fighting one another again as adults.

Cromwell went to Cambridge University but had to leave in less than a year because his father died suddenly. He later studied law in London. He ran the family farm but in 1628 he also became the Member of Parliament for Huntingdon and this was when he came to dislike the way in which England was being ruled by King Charles I.

Cromwell was a strong Puritan and a brave soldier — in one battle his horse was shot and killed under him. He chose his soldiers carefully and trained them well. He taught them how to clean their weapons and care for their horses and he disciplined his men, so that although life was hard, they respected him and followed his orders.

During the war Cromwell found himself on the opposite side to some of his relatives, including old Sir Oliver, his uncle. On one occasion Cromwell's soldiers had to search Sir Oliver's house while uncle and nephew stood talking together outside as if nothing was happening.

Cavaliers* and Roundheads* were the names given to the two sides in the Civil War. The King's men were called Cavaliers which comes from the Spanish word *caballero* meaning 'gentleman'. The King's fighters were gentlemen with beautiful, expensive clothes and long hair. Their hands were white and soft as they had never used them for hard work and most of them came from rich families. The other side laughed at them saying they looked like women.

The Parliamentarian army was made up of the middle classes and tradesmen. They had their hair cut very short, which was the fashion of this class in the 1640s. Very short hair makes heads look rounder and so the King's supporters called the enemy Roundheads. However, officers, such as Oliver Cromwell, wore their hair as long as any Royalist*.

At the beginning of the war the King had most support in the north and west of the country while Parliament was in control in London and in the southern and eastern parts of England.

Few of the King's soldiers had been trained to fight — there was not enough time. They fought with muskets* and pikes* which they could not use very well and the horsemen wore very heavy armour* so it took them a

Roundhead and Cavalier

long time to get on their horses and made fighting difficult. Many of the horses were old and heavy and could not move very fast. The muskets were heavy and complicated to use — it took almost five minutes to put in a bullet and prepare the gun for shooting. Even more of a problem was the fact that nobody was really interested in the fighting and a lot of the soldiers did not even know what they were fighting for. Many simple village people only took part because it was something different to do. Fighting, for them, was more fun than working in the fields or doing nothing all day.

Oliver Cromwell realised that unless Parliament succeeded in getting together an army that really wanted to fight and believed in what Parliament was fighting for, they would never win. Law and order in the towns and villages was breaking down and people were fighting each other in the streets. They were breaking shop windows and stealing food and anything else they wanted. Neither side was happy with this situation.

In those days of poor communication nobody knew what was happening in the other parts of the country. The roads were very bad, especially in winter when they were covered in mud, and so it was difficult for news to travel quickly from place to place. Also, it meant that armies could only cover about fifteen kilometres a day and in this type of war each fighting group felt cut off from the rest of the army and the events in the other parts of the country.

On the battlefield itself, nobody could see what was happening as there was so much smoke from the big guns. It was almost impossible to see or breathe. Some-times there was so much smoke that the armies killed their own men by mistake and they decided that each side should wear different coloured scarves* so that they could recognise each other more easily. The King's army wore red scarves and the Parliamentarian army wore orange.

It was very sad that people who came from the same country and who spoke the same language should be fighting each other. As more soldiers got killed or had their legs blown off by the guns and lay screaming on the battlefield, people began to ask themselves if they should continue fighting. Was it all worth it? What was it all for?

6
From Edgehill to Marston Moor

After the Battle of Edgehill the King's army tried to march to London but Cromwell's men met them and sent them back. So the King stayed in Oxford and the Parliamentarians stayed in London. The Navy supported Parliament and so Parliament had all the ships it needed to control the ports.

Meanwhile, in Holland, Queen Henrietta Maria had sold all her jewels to pay for an army to help the King. She wanted to be with her husband again and she knew that he needed her help. One night she landed with all her men and lots of weapons on a beach in northern England and soon joined her husband in Oxford. However, Charles still felt that they had not enough soldiers, so he brought some English soldiers from Ireland. These men did not want to fight other Englishmen and they left the army and ran away at the first opportunity.

In 1644 the Scottish Presbyterian* army marched into England to help Sir Thomas Fairfax fight the King's army in York. King Charles ordered Prince Rupert to go to York to fight Fairfax. So Prince Rupert and his army and his dog marched north and the armies met in the Battle of Marston Moor in July 1644.

Prince Rupert arrived as it was getting dark. It was an unpleasant evening and the fields were wet. As he thought there would be no fighting that evening, he went into his tent to have supper. Suddenly he heard gunfire and the sound of horses' hooves. Cromwell's army had arrived and the battle began as the rain poured down and thunder crashed. Shouts and screams were heard. Bullets were fired, men pushed their pikes deep into each other's bodies and blood mixed with the rain and the rain with the blood.

At one moment Sir Thomas Fairfax, the leader of the Parliamentarian army, found himself surrounded by the King's men but he quickly removed the scarf which showed him to be one of Cromwell's men (a white scarf for a leader) and succeeded in reaching his own army safely. These coloured scarves were very important for showing on which side the men were fighting, as the soldiers had no uniforms.

When at last the fighting and the rain were over, a large, bright moon shone down on all the dead bodies which were scattered over the field. Four thousand bodies were waiting to be buried.

The Parliamentarians had won, probably because of Cromwell's discipline. His men were trained to obey him, and he made them sing hymns* before each battle. Reading the Bible and praying were also an important part of their day. They were well organised and they believed in the cause* they were fighting for. The King's men, on the other hand, were not even sure they wanted to fight.

Cromwell had been right. His Ironsides — his specially trained soldiers — had succeeded. Parliament now decided to reorganise its whole army in the same way. It was called the New Model Army and was England's first real permanent army. Until that time it had always been necessary to find men when there was a battle or a war to be fought and send them home again afterwards. This meant that the soldiers were usually untrained and unhappy to be away from home and their work in the fields. The New Model Army was the beginning of a professional*, full-time army consisting for the first time of skilled soldiers.

King Charles' army had lost many men. After the Battle of Marston Moor, those that lived were very tired and many had lost an arm or a leg. It was a long, hot summer.

Meanwhile, King Charles was safe at his court in Oxford, many miles from the screams and blood of battle. For a time the situation seemed impossible for him as he had no more money and hardly any men. But Charles' prospects* began to improve when his friend Montrose in Scotland succeeded in gathering a new army together. They marched towards England.

Cromwell was still not a happy man. It was very difficult to know what was happening in other parts of England as, with such bad roads, it took a long time before news got through. He had the feeling that his leaders in other parts of England were not making enough effort. Among the officers above him there was one man whom Cromwell very much disliked — the

Earl of Manchester. Manchester told Cromwell that he didn't know what to do. He said that if Parliament beat the King ninety-nine times, they would still have to obey him but if King Charles beat the Parliamentarians once, they would all be hanged. It seemed he was still afraid of the authority of the King.

`By 1645 most people in England were tired of all the fighting and many of the soldiers just wanted to go home. They seemed to be getting nowhere. Sometimes both sides came together to negotiate and attempt to find a solution* which would satisfy all sides. But King Charles remained determined not to give up his power and insisted on keeping the Church, the throne and his friends.

Charles' men began to quarrel among themselves and they were angry with Charles, complaining that they were never told of his plans. Neither was the King's army the only voice to criticise Charles. His wife was also angry with him. She complained that she had sold her jewels to raise enough money for the army and had even brought men from abroad to fight for Charles. The King, she said, must win the war. The Queen now had nine children and did not want them to grow up in an England torn apart by civil war. So she went to live in France from where she wrote Charles many letters, telling him what mistakes he had made and advising him on how to organise his armies. She was very frustrated* by him because of his indecisiveness*.

The discussions between King and Parliament continued but the King insisted that he must control the army and keep his Church leaders. Cromwell could agree to neither request and eventually decided that the talks were pointless* and leading nowhere. What was needed was action. The Parliamentarian army, led by Cromwell and Fairfax, must set out to destroy the King's armies once and for all.

Queen Henrietta Maria

7
The King is defeated

The Parliamentarian army was now highly organised. The soldiers all wore red coats and were paid good money although a few could not bear the hard discipline and ran away when they had the chance. When Charles's men heard about Cromwell's New Model Army, they were quite frightened. Some decided that they had had enough of fighting anyway and were missing their comfortable houses and good food. A lot of them were not really soldiers — they were gentlemen, unused to living in such rough conditions — so when they heard of the advance of the New Model Army, they left their posts and returned to London. Back in London they were made to pay fines by the Parliamentarians for supporting the King. So the King's men paid their fines and kept out of the fighting.

Charles then went north with Prince Rupert and the army to try to get help from Montrose's army which was on its way to Scotland. On their way they attacked the town of Leicester, killing many of the people, looting* the shops and houses and stealing whatever they wanted. The people of Leicester had not been expecting an attack, especially at night, and were taken by surprise.

Charles was very pleased with his victory and wrote to his wife:

'. . . and we have won a victory at Leicester. Would you believe it, my dearest, they were all asleep! No-one knew we were coming and so it was all quite easy. I realise you have thought sometimes that we were not fighting hard enough. Now I hope you will see that we are winning . . .'

However, while Charles was writing this letter, and hoping that the Queen would now stop criticising him, Fairfax and Cromwell were preparing to attack the King's army at Naseby, a small town just a few miles from Leicester.

This battle was one of the most famous in the Civil War. Charles wanted to take part in it and appeared in a suit* of golden armour but he wasn't allowed to fight in the battle and was told by his officers to keep out of the way while they organised the attacks.

The King and Prince Rupert succeeded in escaping but thousands of their men were taken prisoner and locked up in the churches. Cromwell's army stole the King's weapons and all the letters which Queen Henrietta had written. These letters showed that Charles had plans to bring armies over from Ireland to help him and that he was also planning to buy soldiers from other countries to fight Cromwell. This piece of information turned many of his own men against him. They were shocked at the idea of Charles paying foreign soldiers to fight Englishmen: their patriotic* feelings were stronger than their support for Charles's Royalist cause.

On the other hand, many people were shocked by the behaviour of Cromwell's soldiers after their victories. They often murdered many of the King's soldiers, instead of taking prisoners, and they also attacked the women who moved around the country with the King's army. The soldiers said these women were not important because most of them were Irish and therefore Roman Catholic. Cromwell's soldiers, being Protestants, were automatically against them and felt no guilt* about raping* and torturing the women.

After the Battle of Naseby the King went to live with friends in Raglan Castle in Wales. He used to play bowls* — a game where balls are rolled along on grass — read poetry and go to church and was really quite happy. He was still quite confident that his authority as King, God's representative in England, would save him from the conflict*. His son, Prince Charles, now fifteen years old, had been living in Bristol but he escaped from there when Parliament took control of the city.

However, as the situation developed it became clear that everything was going wrong for King Charles. He quarrelled with Prince Rupert, the whole of Ireland was fighting his army there, and the King's friends in Scotland had been defeated, with Montrose escaping to Norway. King Charles returned to Oxford, knowing he had to find a way to escape. He disguised himself as a servant and he left Oxford and travelled to Nottingham where he surrendered to the Scottish Presbyterian army.

The Scots were not quite sure what to do with Charles so they gave him to the Parliamentary army in return for some money which was owed them and he was taken on horseback* to prison. As he rode through the streets as a prisoner, many people waved their hands and smiled at him. For them he was still a King and always would be. Others, who were sick, tried to touch him hoping to be healed. For them he was still divine.

The Scots had wanted the King to make England accept the Scottish form of religion — Presbyterianism — but Charles refused. So in 1647 the King was taken to Holdenby Hall, in Northamptonshire in central England, which was to be his prison. It was, however, a very pleasant place to live in. It was a large country house and the King spent his time playing games and reading. He still hoped that one day he would be able to return to London and his throne.

Although he was a prisoner, Charles still had a lot of power. Parliament was in a very difficult position. If it was to respect the law, as it claimed the King must do, then it had to respect the King's authority, for the law said Parliament could not govern without the King. The New Model Army, which had fought and won the war, was angry. It wanted Parliament to govern alone and to be rid of the King. That is what its men had fought and died for.

Cromwell was worried. He did not want to get rid of King Charles as the British people were used to having a monarch. The situation could grow worse and he did not want extremists to win the day. He realised it would be difficult to keep the King but things might be even more difficult if Parliament were to get rid of him. On

Oliver Cromwell

the one hand the army might revolt* if the King retained any power. On the other hand, the ordinary people were likely to revolt if Cromwell tried to harm the King in any way.

8
The peace talks

While the King was peacefully playing bowls and reading poetry in a pleasant country house, Parliament was having a difficult time in London. Its Members continued to have bitter arguments with the Army which, now the war had ended, had nothing to do. It seemed that nothing had changed and the men began to ask themselves what they had been fighting for. Cromwell was ill and he was feeling impatient that someone who was in prison could still have so much authority.

King Charles was pleased to hear about the quarrels and problems in London. The quarrels were mainly about religion. The three Protestant groups were against the Catholics, but the Protestants, Puritans and Scottish Presbyterians also quarrelled with each other continuously. Each group had private discussions with Charles offering to support him as King if he would support their form of religion.

Charles wanted to govern as King again. He also wanted to save his much-loved Church of England and his friends and so, although he was prepared to make a few promises to everybody, he didn't really plan to carry out his promises. He believed that once he was back on the throne everybody would have to obey him. In some ways he still had a very naive* faith in the authority of the monarch and the people's respect for this idea.

In 1647 the Presbyterians planned to arrest Cromwell and put him in prison in the Tower of London but Cromwell escaped and met his Army and Fairfax in Newmarket. The King was taken there, too, so that the Army could look after him. They were afraid that the Presbyterian Parliament might try to steal the King back so that they could join with him against Cromwell.

The Tower of London

The meetings at Newmarket were, nevertheless, reasonably* friendly and peaceful. Fairfax actually kissed the King's hand. Discussions took place, the Army leaders asking that people should be allowed to have the kind of Church they wanted. Every citizen should have the right to be a Protestant, a Puritan or a Presbyterian as he wished. That seemed to be the only answer to all the problems. Everyone should be left in peace and perhaps later even the Roman Catholics would be allowed to hold their own religious services in their own homes as long as they promised to support the King and Parliament.

Cromwell believed that Charles would soon be King again and that the King, the Army and Parliament would soon agree. One day Cromwell met the King and all his children and afterwards remarked what a good man he was. It seemed that Cromwell and the King might even be friends and Cromwell was very hopeful that a satisfactory arrangement could be reached.

He was wrong, though, for another war was just around the corner. Cromwell failed to realise the strength of the King's desire to return to absolute power and that he would promise anything to gain time to fight back.

After the negotiations, King Charles was taken to a different prison — Carisbrooke Castle on the Isle of Wight, the little island just off Southampton on the south coast of England. (The Castle can still be seen today.) From Carisbrooke, King Charles encouraged his armies to carry on fighting for him and also attempted to make his enemies quarrel among themselves in order to weaken them. He made lots of promises to the different groups of people, hoping that each group would then want to support him again. He had heard the Royalist armies from Wales and Scotland were planning to rescue him.

Carisbrooke Castle

Obviously Cromwell did not know about these plans and neither did he realise that the promises Charles was making were empty ones. He didn't know that Charles had no intention of keeping them.

Meanwhile General Ireton, Cromwell and King Charles together made a list of suggestions which was presented to the Army and Parliament. These were:

1 The King should be King again.
2 The country should elect* a new Parliament every two years.
3 Protestants should have the freedom they wanted.
4 Parliament should control the Army for the following 10 years.

However there were some people from every political and religious group who did not want to accept these suggestions. Even King Charles refused to say if he would accept them as he did not want to make any decisions while he was waiting to be rescued.

Fighting broke out once more in the streets of London and angry crowds attacked the Houses of Parliament. Cromwell marched his Army into Hyde Park calling for law and order.

However, Cromwell's opinion of King Charles was suddenly changed — by a letter. A man on horseback was taking the letter from King Charles to Queen Henrietta in France when he was stopped by one of Cromwell's men who asked if he was carrying a letter. The man said he wasn't but he got confused when questioned and Cromwell's men searched him. They found the letter and took it to Cromwell.

When Cromwell opened the letter he was filled with anger, for it was clear from the contents that King Charles had been making promises to everybody and that he had lied to Cromwell. King Charles was laughing at the way everybody had believed him. He had written: 'Everybody wants my support but I can't be on everybody's side so I think I'll join the Scots.'

Cromwell immediately decided to fight the King again in order to end the conflict and the struggle for power which was splitting the country in two. In April 1648, the Second Civil War began.

9
The second Civil War

From his prison on the Isle of Wight, Charles had encouraged his supporters not to give up, so the Royalists carried on fighting for their King. But Cromwell was determined that the Royalist army should be destroyed and in any case his Army was both larger and better-trained, so he was certain that he would succeed. The Scottish Presbyterian soldiers marched down to England and, on the border of England and Scotland, met some English Royalists, who joined with them to take over some of the castles.

Meanwhile Cromwell's men were fighting one of King Charles' armies in Wales. Cromwell himself led the attack on Pembroke Castle in Wales and the Royalists soon surrendered. By now Cromwell's soldiers were tired and many were wounded. They wanted to rest but Cromwell ordered them on. Through rain and storms these tired and angry men marched to the north of England. They were so tired when they reached Preston that many of them could hardly stand but Cromwell called in some men and there, at Preston, he defeated the Scottish army. That was almost the end of the Royalists but not quite.

In the summer of 1648, a determined group of Royalists arrived at Colchester in the south east of England and took over the town. Fairfax and his Army arrived the following day and surrounded the town. The Parliamentarians' attack on the town failed so they settled down to wait until the Royalists ran out of food. This siege* lasted for 12 weeks and the men in the town were having to eat their horses, dogs, cats and even rats. They gave up when Fairfax promised not to kill the ordinary soldiers but two of the Royalist leaders were shot outside Colchester Castle.

Colchester Castle

Cromwell had taken many prisoners. Some were shot, others had their heads cut off and some were sold like animals and sent out to the West Indies.

He felt that it was King Charles who had started the Second Civil War and it was because of Charles that the Scots had marched into England. In those days the English saw the Scots as foreigners and each regarded the other with suspicion*, as a dangerous enemy. Even today, although the two countries are united, some Scottish people believe that Parliament in London is not really interested in what happens in Scotland and many Scots want more independence* for Scotland. However, nowadays religion is not a problem. Scottish Presbyterians still exist but it is unlikely that they would wish to fight the English Protestants.

When the Second Civil War ended and Cromwell had returned to London, he decided that Charles, the 'man of blood' as he called him, must go. Cromwell knew that as long as Charles lived, he would always try to be King.

Preparations for the King's trial

The Army had tried to find a way to make Charles king again but a king without any power or authority. Charles, however, was not happy to be king in name only. He wanted power and absolute power that could not be shared. Parliament did not know what to do. It knew that killing Charles would be very unpopular with a lot of the people as many still wanted him to be king.

But Members of Parliament knew that Parliament would have no power while Charles was on the throne. While these discussions continued, Charles, still in prison, was very busy planning to get an army from Ireland to come and rescue him.

General Ireton, Cromwell's right-hand man, was wondering what to do about Parliament. He decided that Charles should be brought to trial and he wanted to get rid of the 'Long Parliament', as it was called and choose a new Parliament that would agree with him. So the Long Parliament was dismissed. In 1640 there had been 552 Members but the new Parliament had only 152 Members and was called the Rump Parliament. (Rump means the tail end or the bottom.) It was given this name because three-quarters of it was missing. The situation was very undemocratic.

General Ireton did not want men in Parliament who wanted to keep the King so one of his men stood at the door of the Houses of Parliament armed with a weapon. He asked each man if they wanted Charles killed and those who said they did not were ordered to leave. Those who remained agreed that they wanted the King to be put on trial. In this way Cromwell forced the Parliament to decide, so that ordinary people would not realise it was really Cromwell's decision. When Cromwell returned to London from a battle in the north he was very pleased to find that Parliament at last agreed with him that Charles should go. He welcomed what he saw as their very wise decision.

The next day King Charles was taken to Windsor

Castle in preparation for his trial. Charles was still sure that one day he would be king again and the streets were crowded with friendly people who shouted: 'Long live the King!' and waved to him as he went past. Many took off their hats to show their respect.

In fact, not every Member of the Rump Parliament wanted the King's death even though General Ireton thought he had successfully kept out those who were against the trial of King Charles. The House of Lords, the upper House which normally has to give its permission before a change in the law is made, was against the trial of King Charles.

Cromwell, however, decided to take no notice of the House of Lords and to go on with the trial. However, no judge would agree to judge the case. Some did not want the King to die, while others were frightened for their own safety if they sent Charles to his death. When the judges refused to take part, Cromwell immediately made some new ones. These were rather unusual judges. Normally in trials there is a jury* of 12 ordinary people who have to consider all the information carefully and then decide who is right. Cromwell's judges, however, were not only judges, they were also the jury, and, as Cromwell had chosen the members of this jury himself, it was quite clear whose side they were on and what decision they would make in the trial.

Finally 135 judges were chosen but only 68 of them appeared. The others were too frightened to show their faces. At last the final preparations for the trial were made and the trial itself could start. Would Cromwell succeed or was the opposition* still too great?

10
The execution of King Charles

Sir Thomas Fairfax, one of Cromwell's generals, did not agree with what Cromwell was doing at the opening of the trial and his wife, Lady Fairfax, shouted angrily from the public gallery*, the place above the court where ordinary people can sit and watch a trial. The chief judge was so afraid that someone might shoot at him from the gallery that he wore a steel hat and armour under his shirt to protect himself from bullets.

King Charles, fashionably dressed in black, behaved with great courage. He was very calm and brave and more and more people began to feel respect for him. He said that the trial was against the law and that he was fighting for the freedom of his people. If power alone, without law, were allowed to make laws, he said, freedom would be lost.

But Charles was found guilty. The time came for the judges to sign their names on the death warrant — the paper which said King Charles should die — but many refused to sign and Cromwell was bitterly angry. Cromwell was sure that God had chosen him and not King Charles as the person to carry out His wishes and nothing could stop him now. He even held his hand

The death warrant of Charles I

firmly over the judges' hands to make them sign but only 59 signatures* appeared on the death warrant.

In January 1649 the King spoke his last words to the people. He had not changed his opinions and still believed that the King should have the power and that only under the King's law could people be free. He said he was dying for the things in which he believed. Then he was taken to be beheaded in public, the only King in English history to be executed like a murderer.

The executioner's axe came down and the King's head was lifted up for everyone to see. Afterwards the executioner made a lot of money for himself as people paid to put their handkerchiefs in the King's blood and some bought pieces of his hair. Later the head was

Charles I at his trial

fastened to the body again and then the body was embalmed*, that is, certain chemicals were put into the body so that King Charles looked young, alive and healthy.

His faithful friends carried the King's body through a snowstorm to St George's Chapel in Windsor where it was buried. They had no church service because Cromwell did not allow them to read from the prayer book. That was the end of King Charles I and the end of the idea which he believed so strongly, that Kings were sent by God to represent Him on earth.

The Commonwealth in danger

After King Charles had been put to death, it was decided that England would never again have a king and there was no longer to be a House of Lords. The new Government was to be called a Commonwealth*.

The Rump Parliament continued to govern and made the decisions but the people did not like what the new government did. Many still wanted to have a King, especially the Scots and the Irish who were sad and angry at Charles' death and refused to accept the new government. Cromwell took his New Model Army to Dublin to force the Irish to obey. Many Roman Catholic priests were murdered, some prisoners were killed and others were sold and taken to other countries. Cromwell and his men took everything they had, looting and stealing through Ireland, burning their houses. Ireland was in ruins. The people were left in hunger, despair and such misery* that even now, 300 years later, the name of Cromwell is still hated in Ireland, and, amongst Catholics, there is a deep suspicion of the English.

Next, Cromwell went to fight the Scots who had said they wanted Prince Charles, the son of Charles I, to be their king. Prince Charles had returned from Holland in 1650 and called together a Scottish Presbyterian army. He was crowned King Charles of Scotland in November 1650.

Cromwell was very worried. He believed his Commonwealth was in danger as Prince Charles wanted to be King of England and the Scots were preparing to march into England. He no longer had his two closest supporters — General Ireton had died in Ireland and Fairfax had had enough of the fighting and had returned to his house in the country.

Cromwell got together the army of Parliament and set off to meet the Scots. He was soon over the border into Scotland and the two armies met at Dunbar. The Scots were beaten but the soldiers who were left met King Charles and they decided to march to England, although they hoped to avoid having to fight Cromwell's army again. Cromwell had moved his army to Perth in the east, so Charles marched down the west side of Scotland to Carlisle. He wanted to get to London and have himself crowned King before Cromwell could stop him. Cromwell heard of the plan and set off after him.

Charles tried to get more soldiers as he went but the English were tired of war and very few joined him.

When he arrived at Worcester, he had only 12,000 men and by this time Cromwell was close behind him with 30,000 trained soldiers. Cromwell divided his soldiers into two halves and Charles' army was caught between the two. Charles' men fought bravely but were beaten.

Charles himself escaped from the battle of Worcester and rode to the house of the Gifford family who gave him shelter. There he decided to escape to France. Charles changed into old workman's clothes, had his hair cut short and rubbed mud onto his face so that he no longer looked like a king. Then, with a servant of the Gifford family called Richard Penderel, he set out on foot. Cromwell's men were all around them. Houses were being searched and there were soldiers on all the roads but Richard Penderel cleverly suggested that Charles should climb a large tree to hide. The soldiers searched below while the King looked down on them from the branches above. A little later the King had to hide in a chimney while Cromwell's men searched the house he was in. They looked up the chimney but Charles was hiding a long way up and they did not find him.

Charles was a tall man so it was decided that he should ride a horse to Bristol in order that his height would not be noticed and give him away. From there he could get a ship to take him to France. A young lady named Mistress Lane rode on the horse behind Charles, as in those days young ladies often rode behind a servant. In one village they rode past some of Cromwell's soldiers but were not stopped.

Charles could not get a ship at Bristol so went on to Brighton and sailed from there in 1651. He had spent 45 days running away from Cromwell's men and now went to France to plan his next attempt to become king of England. He lived in France for a time but Cromwell, who now knew where he was, thought this was too close to England. It would be much too easy for Charles to return to England and be crowned king. So Cromwell persuaded the French King to send Charles away and he went to live in what is now Belgium.

11
The Lord Protector

Cromwell's supporters gave him a wonderful welcome when he returned to London after winning the Battle of Worcester. Ireland was powerless, the Scots had been defeated and Charles had run away. It seemed that Cromwell and his Rump Parliament could now govern England as they wanted.

However this was not to be. Cromwell thought the Rump Parliament would try to govern Britain in a fair and just way but it was more interested in keeping its own power than in making England a happy, peaceful country again. Cromwell also had other problems to deal with.

He was angry with the Dutch because Holland would not recognise his new government. Also, Prince Rupert, who had been King Charles I's closest adviser, had gathered some Royalist supporters together and they were sailing around Britain with fighting ships waiting for a chance to attack. He could not forgive Cromwell for killing King Charles I. Cromwell got some ships together and attacked these Royalists, separating Rupert's ships and forcing them to sail away in different directions. Cromwell was as dangerous on sea as he was on land.

The Dutch navy was also ready to attack the English and the leader had tied a large brush to his ship to show he would sweep the English from the seas. When the Dutch navy saw Cromwell's large and determined naval force, it quickly sailed back to Holland without attempting to attack.

Now it was time for Cromwell to take control of the Parliament. He told Members that it had sat for too long and a new Parliament was needed. However, the Members did not want to give up their power even though they had not been elected to the Parliament democratically. They had been given power by Cromwell but were now unwilling to surrender that power to him.

The next day Cromwell took 30 soldiers with him to Parliament and made them wait outside the House while he went in and sat down quietly in his usual place. After a while he stood up and once more told Members that this Parliament had sat for long enough and it was time for a change. One Member stood up to protest but Cromwell did not give him a chance to speak. He called in his soldiers. As soon as the Members of Parliament saw the thirty men with their long pikes, they ran out of the House fearing for their lives and Cromwell locked the doors behind them.

Never had Parliament dismissed itself so quickly. Now the only government left was Oliver Cromwell who stood alone in the House. The King was dead and Parliament had just been dismissed by Cromwell, but he did not want to govern alone. He did not want to be king. He wanted a Parliament but a good Parliament. He was afraid, however, that if the people of England were allowed to elect the new Parliament, they would choose a Royalist Parliament which would mean that there would soon be a king again.

Cromwell could not accept that so he decided that the Army should choose the new Parliament. The Army chose Puritans and their leader had the strange name of Praise-God Barebones. So the new Parliament became known as Barebones' Parliament. With this Parliament the Puritan way of life continued. People had to behave in a serious manner and were not allowed to enjoy themselves because it was sinful* and against the laws of God. They were forced to be religious and good.

Here are some examples of Puritan laws:

1 No-one is allowed to go for a walk on Sundays.
2 Christmas dinner may not be eaten.
3 It is forbidden to laugh on Sundays.
4 All theatres must be closed.
5 No sports may be played on Sundays.

A young girl who was found mending her dress on a Sunday after having torn it on her way to church was put in the stocks* as a punishment. The stocks were a wooden frame used to keep someone a prisoner and were always found on the grass in the middle of the village. The 'criminal' had to sit in his place with his feet through holes in the frame so that he could not escape and people in the village were allowed to throw eggs and fruit or stones at him.

Unfortunately, Barebones' Parliament was no better

A criminal in the stocks

than the Rump Parliament. They governed only in their own interests, not in the interests of the people. Cromwell was angry and disappointed and told the Members they did not know how to govern. He said they should leave. Cromwell had again taken a small army with him to the House in case Barebones would not go and once more Parliament was dismissed.

The Army then suggested that Cromwell himself should govern England and so, in 1653, Oliver Cromwell became Lord Protector of England. He was now 53 years old and he still had no wish to govern alone, having no ambitions to become a king or have absolute power. He hoped that someone would soon find a better way to run the country peacefully. He then declared that his power was now civil and not military* and exchanged his red army uniform for an ordinary black suit as a symbol* of the fact that he was no longer a soldier.

Oliver Cromwell was not happy as Lord Protector. He felt that something was wrong and knew that there were a lot of people in England who did not want him to govern the country. Many resented* the Puritan laws and although they realised that King Charles I had been corrupt*, they felt it was better to have a king in charge of the country rather than an 'ordinary' man like Cromwell who was not from a royal family. Many people remained traditional* in their views, uninterested in a republican* form of government.

12

Cromwell is dead — Long Live the King!

As Lord Protector of England, Cromwell made peace with the Dutch and England did a lot of trade with Holland. Many Dutch people came to live in south-east England and helped the English to develop their wool industry.

Spain and England, however, still continued to quarrel. Cromwell sent his ships to trade with countries that belonged to Spain and Cromwell's men also took Jamaica from the Spanish — a rich island because of its sugar.

At home there were many disagreements about money, taxes and the way that religious freedom was limited. Cromwell was more undemocratic, more of a dictator* than Charles I had ever been, and he divided England into eleven military divisions. With over half a million men in his Army at a time when there were only five million people in England, there was one soldier for every ten people. He hoped in this way to keep the people under control.

To keep this Army, Cromwell had to make people pay a lot of money in taxes and the English resented being taxed to pay for an army now that the war was over. Many people were tired of Cromwell, the Army and the Puritans and their laws. More and more people wanted to choose their own Parliament. They felt they had had more freedom under Charles I.

Cromwell's power brought him no happiness and he died in September 1658 after governing England for nine years. Before dying he said his son, Richard, should take his place as Lord Protector after his death. Richard, however, had never been a soldier, had no idea about how to govern a country and had no real desire to take on the responsibility of being Lord Protector.

He soon gave up his position after which there were many rump parliaments which governed badly, quarrelling for most of their short lives. The situation was impossible. The Army and Parliament could not agree. People who had supported the Commonwealth now wanted to see the return of the King, because they felt they needed one person to have absolute power.

Finally, in 1659, General George Monck, the leader of the army in Scotland, brought his army to England. Monck was an ex-Royalist who had served well under Cromwell and his army was well disciplined. He did not want to see England ruled by the Army and its guards. When he arrived in London he found that the rump parliament was sitting again and he supported it against the Army. This meant that for the first time since the war there were more Royalists than Republicans in the parliament and they could influence the decisions.

At last the people were allowed to choose their own government. And they chose the King. They wanted a king and a Parliament made up of both a House of Commons and a House of Lords. They wanted Prince Charles, still the King of Scotland, to return to England. Monck laid down the conditions for Charles' return to the throne which was known as the Declaration of Breda, the name of the place where Charles was staying in Holland.

In May 1660, Charles arrived. Church bells rang, fires were lit, people sang and laughed and danced in the streets. No king had ever had a warmer welcome. Soon after, he was crowned King Charles II.

Charles II

Someone who had remained a true Royalist during the period of the Commonwealth was the Earl of Clarendon. He had kept the young Prince Charles in touch with the Church of England while the Prince was living abroad with his Catholic mother. Now he helped King Charles II give peace to the land. Neither of them allowed the Roundheads to be persecuted as it was important for peace that the King should be accepted by everybody. Only those who had signed the King's death warrant were put to death.

Once again, then, England had a king. But there had been many changes. First, the idea of the Divine Right of Kings had gone for ever. No king would ever again be allowed to be all-powerful and to pretend that his power came from God. Secondly, because of the Civil War, English people had learnt religious tolerance*. They had seen how terrible and frightening the extreme forms of religion were and they had seen Englishmen fighting against Englishmen in the name of religion. Thousands of people had died for religious reasons, and so it was time for more tolerance for peoples' beliefs. As Protector, Cromwell had encouraged religious freedom. Even the Roman Catholics had received kinder treatment under the Protector than they had from Puritan parliaments.

The English also decided there should be no regular army which a monarch might use against the people. The Civil War soldiers were paid off and returned to ordinary life but an exception was made in the case of the soldiers who had marched with General Monck from Scotland; those who had helped to bring back the King.

This regiment* of soldiers remains today. It is called the Coldstream Guards because it was at the village of Coldstream that they crossed the River Tweed into England on their famous march to London.

Perhaps most important for the political future of England was that people from that time on were allowed to choose their own Parliament. Nothing could be done without the permission of Parliament and so no king or queen could become too powerful.

The wars stopped and people turned away from violence. From then on they wanted slow, not sudden, changes. Some years later the system of government as we know it in England today was set up and many other countries have copied it.

This system gives people freedom under the law. The ideas were originally worked out and tested during the first and most important English revolution — the Civil War. If the English Civil War had never happened, the system of government in England today would have been completely different.

13
Life in the 17th century

The most important person in every 17th century family was the father. Children were brought up in a very firm way. They had to stand when speaking to their parents and all children, even princesses, were beaten to 'correct' them if they did not behave in the right manner. Before the Civil War fathers hardly knew their children but during this time they grew closer and children were often given special names by their parents, known as 'nicknames'. Sir Thomas Fairfax, for instance, while fighting in the Civil War, sent messages of love to 'little Moll', his daughter, whose real name was Mary. And some people at this time began to think it might be wrong to beat children and suggested that kindness might be a preferable method of improving their behaviour.

Family groups were often very large. Women had a lot of babies, though often many died, and aunts, uncles and grandparents sometimes lived with the family, as did a large number of servants in rich families. Even shopkeepers had one or two servants.

Parents arranged the marriages of their children and sometimes children were married at a very young age.

Girls were allowed to marry at the age of 14 though when such young children married they did not live together until they were older. Later in the century such young marriages grew less common but, even so, the daughters of rich families were expected to marry between the ages of 16 and 20. The Church taught that it was wrong to force a girl to marry a man she really disliked but parents would often try hard to persuade her to do so.

Rich fathers gave their daughters a present, known as a 'dowry', of land or money when the girl married and the fathers of sons considered the size of a girl's dowry when arranging a marriage for their son. Even poor girls took some sort of present to their new home, usually something to be used in the house. Poor people were usually older when they married as it took young men some time before they could earn enough to keep a wife and family. Everyone in a family, rich or poor, suffered if the father, the head of the family, died and could no longer provide for them.

The rich lived comfortably in beautifully designed new houses — people today have to pay a lot of money to buy a 17th century house. They also had beautiful furniture (which people today also love to own). But the children of the period did not live so comfortably. They spent most of their time in a special group of rooms in the house called the 'nursery', which contained much simpler furniture. Until they were six or seven years old, children were looked after in their nursery by a nurse and they only visited their parents at particular

Cromwell's house at Ely

times or when called for. When they were seven, boys went on to school or had a private teacher at home and girls either had a private teacher or a lady companion to look after and educate them.

Both young boys and girls in rich families wore long dresses. Babies were wrapped in strips of cloth so that they could not move their arms and legs — it was thought it would stop them from hurting themselves. They then went into long dresses and wore close-fitting caps on their heads in the house so that they did not catch cold. Boys did not begin to wear trousers until they were about six years old. These trousers were, of course, different to those worn by boys in England today and came down only to the knee. Younger boys wore their hair down to their shoulders but the older ones wore long, false hair which we call a 'wig'.

Today in England, not many people wear special black clothes when someone has died except for on the day the dead person is buried. Young children now never wear black because someone has died but they did in the 17th century. At a time when so many people in a family died young, the children must often have been dressed in black.

The children of Puritan families always wore plain, dark clothes, of course, even those whose families were rich.

Rich people generally ate well although simple, plain food was given to their children. They had meat, plenty of fresh fish all year round, some vegetables, including potatoes which had been introduced from America, bread, cakes and fruit. They also had sugar from the West Indies.

The poor people did not eat so well but their food was better than that of most other poor people in Europe — indeed, at this time many poor French people starved to death.

About one boy in every two or three, and far fewer girls, learnt to read and write. This was an improvement on the 16th century. Some people thought that if the poor could read and write they would stop being satisfied with their lives as workers. Others, however, felt that being able to read and write would make the lives of the poor more interesting and they would then be happier. Some wealthy men who believed this, left money after they had died to pay for a teacher for the sons of the local poor.

After learning to read and write in a small local school, some lucky boys whose parents had enough money to pay or some who were given free places, went to a higher school known as a 'grammar' school. Oliver Cromwell, as a boy, went to a grammar school in Huntingdon. Often grammar schools were very small, with only one teacher. Some sons of wealthy families went away to boarding school which is a school where the pupils live as well as do lessons. They go home only during the holidays. Two fashionable and expensive boarding schools for boys at the time were Eton and Westminster, and these two very good schools still exist today. Parents still have to pay for their children to go to them and they are still expensive.

Many rich boys went to university at Oxford or Cambridge, which were the only two universities in England at that time, and some poor boys went on to university from grammar school after passing an examination.

Most girls were taught at home, if they had any lessons, but there were also some boarding schools for girls. The daughters of wealthy parents sometimes went to these boarding schools where they studied a few subjects and learnt to sing and dance. However, a private teacher was usually employed at home for the daughters of the rich and some girls received a very good education. Girls did not, however, go on to university.

The children of the rich began their lessons before the

age of five but those from poorer families had to work from that age and those in the country helped with farm work. Girls learnt to milk cows and make butter and cheese. Boys and girls also worked as servants in rich people's houses. Girls would cook and help look after the house and boys might help in the kitchen or help look after the horses. If they were attractive, boys might even be taught to sing and play a musical instrument to entertain the family. Servants worked very hard for long hours with no regular free time or holidays but they lived with the families for whom they worked and received food and clothes as well as their small wages.

Some children worked in coal-mines and in industry. Down in the mines they helped carry the coal. Industries in England at the time included paper-making, silk-making and ship-building. Older boys from families with some money could train to learn the skills of a trade. Such a boy would usually begin his training at about the age of twelve and train for seven years. The boy's family had to pay the tradesman a certain amount of money to take the boy who went to live with the tradesman and was fed by him and sometimes given clothes. A few girls also learned a trade such as making hats and dresses for wealthy ladies.

The game of football was popular with boys in the 17th century but it was a very different game from the one played today. It was more like a fight than a game and it was often played through the streets. It was a favourite game of Oliver Cromwell and he played it a lot when he was a student at Cambridge University. Other

sports which people enjoyed in the 17th century were cock-fighting (a cock is a male chicken) and setting dogs to attack bears. With cock-fighting, cocks were trained to fight and the fight would continue until one cock died. Setting dogs on to bears happened in places called 'bear-gardens'. However, even at that time, both these sports were considered cruel by many.

Everyone enjoyed fairs which were larger events in the 1600s than they are now. St Bartholomew's Fair, which was held every August in Smithfield, London, lasted about two weeks. As well as lots of different things for sale at these fairs, there were entertainments such as performing animals. Unlike now, London had such cold winters then that sometimes the River Thames froze over with ice. Then Frost Fairs were held on the frozen Thames.

The theatre has always been a popular form of entertainment in England, the exception being during the rule of Parliament when Oliver Cromwell closed all theatres. The Puritans did not approve of the theatre. But, even then, people gave private performances so that when King Charles II, who loved the theatre, became King of England, the public had not forgotten the plays they enjoyed and the theatre became popular once more. It was at this time that it became respectable for women to act on the stage (before that time boys had always acted the parts of women). King Charles' lover, Nell Gwynne, was an actress. Several important writers of plays lived during this period, for instance, Sheridan, Congreve and Wycherley.

Religion was an important part of life in the 17th century and families said prayers together every morning and evening and the children would read from the Bible. It was necessary for everyone to belong to the Church of England but, of course, some secretly belonged to other religions. Every family should have gone to church at least once on Sunday but poor people did not always go. Probably they did not have clothes which they thought good enough to wear.

Although it was forbidden to belong to the Roman Catholic church, many people did, and rich Roman Catholic families kept their own priests in their houses. There were lots of places in the houses in which priests could hide if the house was searched by the King's men. Catholic children were sometimes sent abroad to be taught in Catholic schools.

Many young men from wealthy families spent some time travelling abroad in Europe to improve their education. In the early part of the century, boys were sometimes sent abroad to learn to become soldiers with the English soldiers who were fighting in other countries. At the age of seventeen, Thomas Fairfax had been sent abroad by his father to learn to be a soldier in this way. Poor boys only travelled abroad as soldiers when their army was fighting in a foreign country or if they went to sea.

In the middle of the century the sons of the wealthy were sent on what is known as the 'Grand Tour' with a private teacher. They travelled through France and Italy to learn the language and to study the paintings and buildings and manners of the country. They also had private teachers abroad to teach them such things as language, dancing and music. These tours were very expensive and the boys had to write to their fathers regularly to tell them what they were doing.

For poor boys who chose to go to sea, life was hard and dangerous. Sometimes such boys were made to join the Navy and fight wars. A lot of boys who went to sea never returned alive but there was a chance of doing well and making money.

Some poor people tried to improve their lives by going to live in North America. Poor children, in particular, were sent. Money was found to send them and buy them clothes and food on the journey. They were sent to learn a trade and then be given a piece of land at the age of twenty-one. It must have been very frightening for people making that long journey to a new land and especially so for those children who were sent without their families. It took two or three months to sail to North America (or New England) from England. In the early days, over fifty of the 'Pilgrim Fathers' who sailed to New England in a ship called the *Mayflower* in 1620, died of the cold during their first winter there.

Of course, some foreigners also came to live in England at this time, mostly Protestant families escaping from Roman Catholic countries. Many of these were skilled in a trade and soon found work in English towns. Others taught the French language to English children.

During the period of the Civil War, of course, life

was difficult for many people, both poor and rich. In the early days some boys found war exciting and eagerly became soldiers but many men were killed leaving no-one to look after their families. When the Royalists took Bolton, a town in Lancashire, in 1644, someone wrote at the time that the soldiers left almost 60 women without their husbands and hundreds of children without their fathers. He wrote that only a few women and children were all that was left, without anything to eat, hardly any beds to sleep on or cups to drink from.

Thomas Fairfax almost lost his own family during the war. He was attacked by some Royalists one day when riding with his wife, his five year old daughter, Moll and her nurse. His wife, Lady Fairfax, was caught and taken prisoner by the Royalists but Fairfax himself, though hurt, escaped with Moll and her nurse. They rode for 20 hours with Moll sitting on her nurse's horse until Moll fainted. Fairfax left her at a house, thinking she would die but, in fact, she recovered and joined her father later. Fortunately Lady Fairfax was returned by the Royalists and she joined her family once more.

14
Who's who in the English Revolution

Who were the main people on each side?

King Charles's supporters:

His army: the Cavaliers, or Royalists.

The Church of England, led by Archbishop Laud who had written the prayer book that everyone had to use.

The rich farmers and landowners.

Many poor people who did not want changes in their world and wanted a King to tell them what to do.

Queen Henrietta Maria, Charles's French wife. She was a brave and strong woman who helped her husband, though she often thought he was stupid and indecisive.

Duke of Buckingham, a close friend of Charles for many years. He had many enemies and was murdered.

Thomas Wentworth, the Earl of Stafford, who advised Charles what to do and brought an army from Ireland to fight the Scots. He was later executed.

Prince Rupert, the King's nephew. He fought through the civil war and helped to bring Charles II to the throne in 1660.

Prince Charles, the King's son, who went abroad when his father was executed. He became King of Scotland in 1650 and King of England in 1660. He was defeated by Cromwell at the battle of Worcester and had to hide from Cromwell's soldiers.

Parliament's supporters:

Their army: the Roundheads.

The Puritans and the Presbyterians from Scotland.

Many of the tradesmen, bankers, lawyers and shopkeepers, who were becoming rich and wanted more power for the middle classes.

Oliver Cromwell, the main fighter for Parliament. He created the New Model Army. Later he became the Lord Protector of England.

John Eliot, the leader of Parliament who died as a prisoner in the Tower because Charles didn't like him.

John Hampden, a member of Parliament who was against the Ship Tax.

John Pym, who fought for more power for the Parliament.

Thomas Fairfax, one of the army leaders.

Henry Ireton, one of Cromwell's generals, who fought at the battle of Naseby. He married Cromwell's daughter.

Richard Cromwell, the son of Oliver, who became the Lord Protector of England when his father died in 1659. He did not like the job and soon gave it up, so that Parliament and the army could run the country.

Exercises

Comprehension

Chapter 1

1 Why did Charles wear two shirts to his execution?
2 What did the Divine Right of Kings mean?
3 Why did many people not like the Catholic Church?
4 What happened to the Protestants at the time of Mary Tudor?
5 What did the Puritans believe?
6 What did Guy Fawkes do?

Chapter 2

1 Who did Charles marry?
2 What was John Eliot?
3 What was Ship Money?
4 Why did the Pilgrim Fathers leave England?

Chapter 3

1 What did Thomas Wentworth do?
2 Who was John Pym and what did he do?
3 Why did the Scots take money from King Charles?
4 Why did Charles take soldiers to the Houses of Parliament?

Chapter 4

1 Why did Charles abandon the throne?
2 Who was Prince Rupert?
3 Why did Charles not stay at Hull?
4 Who won the battle of Edgehill?

Chapter 5

1 Why did Oliver Cromwell leave university early?
2 What did he do before he became an MP?
3 Why was fighting difficult at this time?
4 Why was communication very slow?

Chapter 6

1 How did Charles pay for his new army?
2 Who did Prince Rupert fight at Marston?
3 How did Fairfax escape?
4 Why did Cromwell dislike the Earl of Manchester?

Chapter 7

1 Why did many of Charles' men run away?
2 What did his soldiers do in Leicester?
3 What did Cromwell's soldiers do after the battle of Naseby?
4 Where was the king kept in prison?

Chapter 8

1 Why did both sides have meetings at Newmarket?
2 What did the different Protestant groups offer Charles?
3 What happened to Ireton's list of suggestions for change?
4 Why did Cromwell change his mind about Charles?

Chapter 9

1 Who joined with the Royalists?
2 What happened in Preston?
3 What happened in Colchester in 1648?
4 What did Cromwell decide at the end of the second Civil War?

Chapter 10

1 Why, according to Charles, was it wrong for him to be killed?
2 How did Cromwell make the judges sign the death warrant?
3 How was Charles executed?
4 Why did the Irish come to hate the English?

Chapter 11

1 Why was Cromwell angry with the Dutch?
2 What did Prince Rupert try to do?
3 How did Cromwell dismiss the Parliament?

4 Why did many people not like the government of Cromwell?

Chapter 12

1 Why was Cromwell unpopular?
2 What happened when he died?
3 How did ordinary people feel at the return of Charles II?
4 What did English people learn from the Civil War?

Chapter 13

1 What is a nickname?
2 How were the children of rich people educated in the 17th century?
3 What did the children of poor people do?
4 Name two sports that were popular in the 17th century.

Writing

1 Imagine you are a Royalist soldier and describe the battle of Edgehill in which you have just taken part. Describe what you could see and hear on the battlefield.
2 Imagine you have gone back to the seventeenth century in a time machine — describe what you think life was like then.
3 Imagine you are King Charles before he was executed. Write a letter to your wife explaining why you started the war and how you feel now.

4 What do you think about the idea of a King controlling the country? Would you be a Royalist or a Republican? Write an essay explaining why you think this.
5 Write an essay explaining why you think religious tolerance is important in the world.

Activities

1 Why did Protestants first break away from the Catholic Church? Look in your library for a book that explains this and write a short history of the conflict.
2 Find out more about the Guy Fawkes plot and re-tell the story in your own words; find out how it is remembered today in Britain.
3 Try to find out what happened to the Pilgrim Fathers when they left England. Where did they go, how did they get on and what problems did they have?
4 The siege at Colchester lasted 12 weeks. Find out about sieges in your own country's history and write a description of one.
5 The English Revolution changed the way that England was organised and governed. Find out about the English government and what the Queen does and make a comparison with the system in your own country.

Language practice

1 Fill in the gaps in this text using new words from the glossary and the text;

> The people of England ——— having Cromwell as the Lord ——— over them because he was more of a ——— than Charles and tried to make people live a ——— life. He stopped them doing ——— things like laughing on Sundays and made them pay extra ——— to pay for the army. Many people wanted their ——— back, as he had ——— power as a ——— right from God and they were happy to ——— him.

2 Look at this example:

> The King said that he had been in favour of religious freedom for Catholics but now he had changed his mind.

> What the King actually said was this:

> 'I was in favour of religious freedom for Catholics but now I have changed my mind'

When someone's speech is reported, it is put into the past tense or the past perfect tense (if it was already in the past). Now report these sentences in the same way:

1 Cromwell said 'I thought the King was a good man but he has lied.'
2 Henrietta said 'You have disappointed me because you can't win any battles.'

3 Rupert said 'I went to Holland to get some ships but Cromwell's ships were better.'
4 Charles said 'I was sent to govern England by God and so it is wrong to put me on trial.'
5 General Ireton said 'The people have suffered a lot. They want to have peace again.'

Glossary

abandon   To leave, often in a hurry, because of danger.

Aldermen   The important men in the government of a town.

anaesthetic   A type of drug used to put people to sleep when they have an operation in hospital.

armour   Metal clothing to protect you from weapons.

Archbishop   The leader of the Church, either for one part of the country or the whole country.

authority   The power of someone who is above someone else.

axe   A sharp metal weapon, also used for cutting down trees.

(to) behead   To cut off someone's head.

(to) betray   To fail to be true and faithful; to sell your country to its enemies in some way.

Bible   The holy book of God.

block   A piece of wood that people put their heads on when they are going to be beheaded.

bowls   A game where balls are rolled along the grass.

cause   The things about which people are fighting; what they believe in.

Catholic   The Roman Catholic Church is the Christian church controlled from Rome by the Pope.

cavaliers   Gentlemen; a name for Charles' supporters.

cellar   The part of a house that is under the ground.

Christian   A person believing in Jesus Christ.

civil   a) Not military — connected with ordinary people.

b) Civil War is when two halves of a country fight each other.

Commonwealth   Cromwell's name for his new form of government, meaning 'for the good of everybody'.

conflict   A fight or disagreement.

(to) consist of   To contain, be made of.

corrupt   Not honest; using power for your own advantage.

(to) descend   To come down.

dictator   A person with absolute power, usually cruel and corrupt.

disguised   Made to look like someone else.

(to) dismiss   To send away.

divine   Sent by God.

division   The parts of something that has been divided.

Earl   A person like a Lord with a royal title.

(to) elect   To choose a government or parliament.

embalmed   Dead bodies are embalmed, that is, kept fresh with chemicals.

(to) execute   To kill someone as a punishment.

executioner   The man who kills people for the government.

extremist A person who has extreme ideas and is considered dangerous.

faithful Someone who always supports and helps his friend.

frustrated Angry because you can't get what you want.

furious Very angry.

gallery A balcony; a place where you can go in a court or Parliament to look down and listen to what is happening.

(to) govern To run a country.

guilt The feeling that you have done something wrong.

horseback On the back of a horse.

hymn A religious song.

indecisiveness Not being able to make a decision.

independence The state of being free, not needing anybody.

jury The twelve ordinary people who sit in a court with a judge and decide if a person is guilty or not.

(to) loot To steal and rob in wartime.

military Connected with the army.

monarch The king or queen.

musket An old-fashioned type of gun.

naive Believing simple ideas.

(to) negotiate To talk about a disagreement and try to decide on an agreement for both sides.

opposition Disagreement with an idea.

parliament The place where the government of the country is organised.

patriotic   Having feelings of love towards your country.

(to) persecute   To punish people because you disagree with them.

persecution   The punishment.

petition   A piece of paper on which people sign their names to show they agree or disagree with something.

pike   An old-fashioned weapon; the end was sharp and you stuck it into people to kill them.

Pilgrim Fathers   A group of Puritans who went to America to escape from persecution.

pointless   Without reason.

Pope   The leader of the Roman Catholic Church.

Presbyterian   The Scottish Protestant Church.

prince   The son of a king.

princess   The daughter of a king.

professional   When you do something as your full-time job.

prospects   Chances for the future.

Protestant   Someone disagreeing with the Catholic Church.

Puritans   Very serious, religious group of Protestants.

rack   A machine for torturing people by stretching their bodies until their bones break.

rape   A crime where a man forces a woman to have sex with him.

reasonably   To a certain extent; quite.

regiment   A group of soldiers living and working

together (each regiment has its own name).

reign   The time that a king or queen remains on the throne.

relatively   'He's a relatively good footballer' means he's quite good when compared to the others.

republican   Someone who believes in a republic, a country that has no monarch.

(to) resent   To be angry and bitter because someone makes you do something you don't want to do.

revolt   When the people of a country fight against the King, parliament or other authority.

Roundheads   A name for the supporters of Cromwell.

royalists   People who believe in the monarchy.

scarf   A piece of cloth you put round your neck to keep warm.

(to) shiver   To shake with cold.

siege   An attack on a town, where the army sits outside the town and waits until the people run out of food.

signature   When you sign your name you write your signature.

sinful   Wrong in the eyes of the church; against the wishes of God.

solution   The answer to a problem.

stocks   A wooden frame that criminals were put into as a punishment. They could not move and people threw things at them.

(to) surrender   To give up fighting and go to your enemy.

suspicion   The feeling that someone is going to do wrong to you; the opposite of trust.

symbol   A picture, or a person, or a word that carries the meaning of an idea in it.

temporarily   For a short time.

throne   The chair that a king sits on.

tolerance   Giving other people freedom to do or think what they want.

(to) torture   To make people suffer pain, in order to make them give secrets, or give up fighting.

traditional   The old way of doing things; against changes.

Treasury   The part of the government that deals with money and taxes.

warrant   A piece of paper that allows you to do something.